ORLANDO

his birth, adventures, travels,
narrow escapes from death, and
eventual mysterious disappearance

prosit

The Orlando Poems

GEORGE MACBETH

THE
ORLANDO
POEMS

MACMILLAN

SBN boards: 333 13109 6
SBN paper: 333 13311 0

First published 1971 by
MACMILLAN LONDON LTD
London and Basingstoke
Associated companies in New York Toronto
Dublin Melbourne Johannesburg & Madras

Printed in Great Britain by
THE BOWERING PRESS
Plymouth

CONTENTS

THE ORANGE POEM

Not very long ago
One morning
I sat in my orange room
With my orange pencil
Eating an orange.

This,
I began to write,
Is the orange poem.
I shall become known
As the orange poet

For inventing
And first writing
The original
Perfect
And now famous

ORANGE POEM
Which this is.
Having written which
In my orange room
With my orange pencil

I turned over a new leaf
Which this is.
Meanwhile,
Inside the orange poem
A small man

With an orange pencil
Sat in an orange room
Eating an orange.
This, he began to write,
Is the orange poem.

I

ORLANDO GETS GOING

THE ORLANDO STORY

1

Prologue.

The Orlando Story, starring
Marlon Brando opened
> last Saturday

at all local cinemas.

It is very gory.

1b

Footnote.

One day Orlando met a man
with a dog
on a ladder.
> Why are you taking him upstairs?

Orlando asked.
> Whereupon, the man dropped

his dog in a well.

2

Chapter Two.

Orlando is now much older.
He lives with his mother and two
children in a hot-house
> full

of rhododendrons.
> Once a week

they take the sécateurs
to his primitive painters.

3

In Chapter Three

Orlando discovers the seeds of paradise, a
new form of drug
                        offering
aphrodisiac pleasures
eternal youth
and a fish-finger taste.
                              Later, he gets stuffed.
Finally, there is a sea-battle
where a whale is eaten
by a crab.
                  Orlando then goes home, coughing.

4

For all those (few I guess)
wanting to hear more about Orlando

PULCI COMICS INC.

offer a weekly three-part serial
entitled
              Where to Get Your News of Orlando
or
A Fresh Look at Our Dream-boy.

5

Sequel.

One night I was walking home late
from the station, when I saw (*deus ex machina*)

          Orlando,

huge white wings, glossy triangles of fur :

Orlando, I cried

and he saluted me with a hoot,
as he passed away for ever into the darkness.

ORLANDO FOR THE BIRDS

1

Yes, well, actually
that was just the synopsis.

Orlando really went on
for another forty-nine cantos,
a few of them in heroic couplets.

At one point,
exuding an air of melons,
and pausing at a careless comma,

HE TOOK OFF
and glanced around the rafters for several minutes
bat-wise.

2

Orlando was quite a lot of birds
at one time :

he had a go at the quetzal

OWA OWA OWA OWA OWA

(real Mexican stuff that)

woodpecker

TICK TOCK TICK TOCK TICK TOCK

and quite a few more
like

sparrow, blackbird, robin
cock of the rock
and

SHSHSH

I think I hear him still
warbling away like a nightingale
in the back of Canto 35.

3

How good it is to be alive,
hearing the cry of the golden-crested
Orlando

and still with all one's faculties
in the year of our Lord —

My God,
he's pecked the head off
my lamp-post.

4

Orlando sidles off,
spitting blood
like any other vulture.

B

TO MIX YOUR ORLANDO

1

    take two table-spoonsful
of bi-carbonate of soda,
a pinch of salt, and
    three cloves :

    shake well for three minutes,

light fuse,
keep well back, and

    HELLO, EVERYONE

    I am Orlando,
the new instant soufflé.

    Eat me, and die.

2

    Those wishing
to take home a trial packet
    of Orlando Draining Fluid

    should contact our representative,
Mr Fizz, in the foyer.

    MONEY BACK IF NOT SATISFIED

3

Not Satisfied

    Wish *my* back
was made of money.

I'd wash it in
liquid honey, not

ORLANDO DRAINING FLUID

Smelly old stuff.

HOW THE ORLANDO POEMS CAME TO BE

1

One day when Orlando
was cleaning out the attic

he came on an old rusting bucket.

At the bottom of the bucket,
wrapped in grease-proof paper,
floated the Orlando poems.

I know, Orlando thought,
I'll write these.

2

A Critical Comment

FITS LIKE A MIRROR

Need a bit
of re-silvering,
but basically

they make a very smooth little

AUTOBIOG

Lucky fellow
you are, sir,

all the glory
and none of the experience.

3

        Orlando wept
with pride
        when he got his review
        in the *New Statesman*

GOD SAVE THE RABBIT POET

massed choirs were made to sing
        for hours
in the Orlando Memorial Stadium.

THE CHARLES DARWIN ORLANDO

1

It is Shotts.
It is 4,000 B.C.

A child is born
in a miner's helmet.

2

PING !

Orlando
springs full grown
from the head of Zeus.

3

Godzilla Versus Orlando

Red in tooth and claw
they struggle together
for several aeons.

Finally, smashing
Godzilla's jaw-bone
on a dead crustacean,

KING ORLANDO

wades out to sea,
beating his breast
and shouting

HERE I COME, FRANKENSTEIN

ORLANDO ATTEMPTS A SECOND CHILDHOOD

1

NAUGHTY ORLANDO

Orlando leans
from his pram
and applies a match

to the tassels of nanny's
night-cap.

2

FIRE FIRE
FIRE FIRE

Orlando wets his nappy,
throws his rattle into the road,
and buries his face
in a piece of coal.

3

Call this a pram?

Feels more like a
burning fiery furnace.

Give us some air, love,
I don't mind a kiss
or two

(on the right extension)
but

SOMEONE ISN'T USING ORLANDO
ASBESTOS AMPLEX

II
ORLANDO'S LIFE IN LONDON

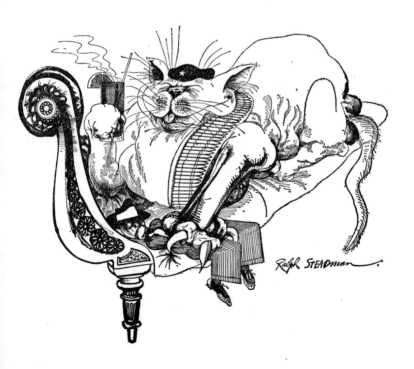

THE PLASTIC ORLANDO BAND

1

Ladies and gentlemen
(if there are any here)
I have asked Orlando
to sing a little song
for our lie-in.

So, a big hand, folks.

2

Clapping.

3

Hello, Yoko,
hello, Jon,
Bless, the bed
that I lie on.

Orlando, Orlandee,
Orlando, re, me, sol, fa.

4

Thank you, Orlando.

That's it, then,
skinheads.

Listen again next week
to *The Plastic Orlando Show.*

ORLANDO IN THE LIBRARY

Orlando reads everything
as if it were braille.

        He doesn't take
a blind bit of notice
when I tell him to stop.

STOP

O no,
he likes to get his teeth into
a nice juicy bit
of scandal
            like :

Mrs Ogre's poems
or
        The Sex Life of Peregrine Butterthorn

(Peregrine writes regularly
        for the *Daily Telegraph,* you
may have read him.)

Anyway,
            Orlando has.

Really got it in for
Peregrine he has.

        When he sees those
uppity sideburns
on the box
            he growls
like a maniac

GRRRRRRRRRR

Orlando was never one
 to conceal his feelings
or sheathe his claws.

WATCH OUT, MR HEATH
TAKE CARE, CHARLES CURRAN
GO HOME, LORD HILL

Orlando is no catholic.

And he doesn't want
to bring the cat back either.

There are enough cats already.

ORLANDO ENTERS THE COMMON MARKET

1

What did we win the war for ?
    (Orlando thought)
as he passed the PANZER DELICATESSEN

    See them everywhere
nowadays.

    BLOODY WOGS
    NIGGERS
    JEW-BOYS

    If I had my way,
I'd flog the ruddy
    lot of them.

    DIRTY BASTARDS

2

    O yes, Mr Eisenstadt,
I think the new Eurovision
    car-wash
is a very flash idea.

    Go a bomb, I'd say.

    Why, only yesterday
I was saying to Mrs Orlando
    (wasn't I, bunny)

    why can't we all let
bygones be bygones
    and realise it's

1970

and we have to lick the arse
of the fucking German people
      whether we

like it or not,
      don't we now ?

This was one of Orlando's
right-wing days.

AN ORLANDO SICKNESS

1

Orlando is turning green.

       I don't know why,
Nobody does.

       It could be the
Irish question, I suppose,
       or just mould.

Anyway, I don't like it.

       Perhaps if we all
shout together
       we could get help.

2

One, two, three :
          HELP

3

       Ah yes, you must be
the new green cat.

       We've been expecting you.

I had a cousin called
       Orlando once.

He went green, too.

HA HA HA HA

Would you mind putting on
this bucket of red pepper?

I know it's a tight fit,
they all are.

4

At this point
Orlando breaks free,
        draws his broadsword
and hacks the psychiatrist to pieces.

Waves of green fill the auditorium.

5

Later, *The Green Kittens*, by
        Kevin Orlando-Holland
is on sale in the foyer
        price 94 new pence.

c

ORLANDO MAKES THE POETRY SCENE

1

Orlando is my Muse.

Whenever I see him
in those tight pink levis
I go all gooey.

Orlando preens his whiskers.

Tight pink levis, eh.

2

The Poet

Sucking her pencil,
she has an orgasm.

Orlando looks on,
turning the handle of the projector.

3

It is blue films day
at the Everyman.

A big queue
composed entirely of women
wraps several times
round the foyer.

Orlando appears
in his tight pink levis.

MMMMMMMMM

       All are satisfied
and return home
      in an orderly manner.

SWEENEY ORLANDO, THE DEMON BARBER

1

Orlando has cut several heads of hair
     in his time :

              Spiro Agnew,
    Yul Brynner, you
    name them.

    It's snip snip
all night long
    in the Orlando residence
    down on Marilyn Boulevard.

2

Interview

    Where's the mike ?

MIKE

    Sorry, he's gone
for dinner.

3

The Life and Death of Radio Three

    Orlando seizes
the dripping razor
and makes off

    down Chapter 15
towards the Emergency exit.

PLEASE SHED YOUR TEARS IN THE
  APPROPRIATE RECEPTACLE

ORLANDO ON THE NORTH CIRCULAR

1

The fire blazes happily
a few inches away
from clothes placed

THOUGHTFULLY

on the fireguard.

Familiar electric wires
trail around a
HOMELY power point.

And on the DEAR TV set, a
delicately balanced goldfish bowl
stands ready to drip water
into the works.

2

CRASH

Orlando picks bits
of goldfish
out of the wreckage.

BLOODY MANIACS

Driving round the bowl
at 120.

3
ALLO ALLO ALLO

What's all this now.

Here's a case for
Chief Inspector Prudential, CID.

THREE QUEERS FOR ORLANDO

1

HIP HIP HIP

All in green
went my love riding
into the Television Centre.

Orlando smoked
so much grass
he couldn't even see him.

2

Funny thing, you
funny thing, you

FUNNY FUNNY FUNNY THING

3

Orlando turns over
three new leaves
on the road to Rugeley.

One of them runs into a drain
and brings a dead pig out
wrapped in cellophane.

One of them sticks
a green carnation
the size of the Ritz
up his arse-hole.

One of them dies, shouting

ANYONE HERE SEEN FLASH HARRY?

III
ORLANDO'S WORLD TOUR

THE POLITICAL ORLANDO

1

Orlando in Chicago

Last year, Orlando
went to Chicago
                for the famous party conference.

        There he met,
one after another,
        three jolly American policemen.

        The first one
hit him with a night-stick
        across the foreskin.

        The second one
spat a wad of half-chewed shag
        all over the blue grass of Illinois.

        The third one
just stood and fingered the butt of his pistol
        like it was some kind of a
surrogate penis.

                After that experience,
Orlando came home,
a sadder but a wiser man.

Next year,
Orlando will go to the moon.

2

Orlando Goes to the Moon

In every particular,
we are the imperialists of the Sea of Tranquillity
        according to Orlando,

or will be,
when he gets there.

Three for the sea-saw :
        the Plain of Jars
        the Bay of Pigs
        and the Sea of Tranquillity

Orlando knows them all,
their qualities,
            and how to put quite a good face
on why the Stars and Stripes
had to be pinned there.

        Quite a story,
how Orlando got his Purple Heart.

3

Orlando in Vietnam

        Now it can be told :

        Orlando is on
a search and destroy mission.

        Over the roof-tops
he goes with his claws out
        in a chopper.

        From a small 7-transistor radio set
he will keep in earshot
        of the top thirty.

                Some of them, a select few,
may even be in there with him,
                wide-eyed
                and bushy-tailed.

                Orlando is facing out
the VCs
eyeball to eyeball.

                If he isn't careful,
Orlando is going to win
another medal.

Orlando will have a
ticker-tape welcome
                back in Yawnsville, Massachusetts,

where the worst that ever happens
is the local dentist
                having his wisdom teeth out.

                Ah me, thought Orlando
(reading this)
                if only a few others,
                naming no names,
had had their wisdom teeth put in !

Orlando is quite a philosopher.

ORLANDO IN THE LAND OF THE RISING SUN

1

An Orlando Transplant

POOR ORLANDO

He has been rejected.

He feels very sad.

2

BE OF GOOD HEART

The American warships
will be here shortly.

Orlando breathes again.

3

1945

Meanwhile,
a small man
with a tight face

commits hara-kiri in a corner.

He failed to hold Okinawa.

STEAMING ORGANS ARE LIFTED TO THE SUN

4

Paper flowers
open in bowls of rice.

Men in rickshaws
are reading Orlando's
latest collection

of *Vampire Tanka*.

5

The clockwork dolphin
mows down the ceiling
with characteristic fervour.

BLOOD BLOOD EVERYWHERE

And not a drop to drink.

Orlando retires to his coffin.

ORLANDO IN TRANSYLVANIA

1

It is a dark
wet night.

The carriage clatters
on the road to the hostelry.

AIAI

Orlando appears,
cloak spread, wings black in the moonlight.

2

Would the owner of
STAKE NUMBER OYF 162F
please come to the moated grange.

There seems to be ketchup
on her clutch pedal.

3

FREE BLOOD SAMPLE

Orlando enters
the Karloff Institute
with some trepidation.

CREAMY BLEEDO NEVER CURED ANYONE

ORLANDO AT THE CONQUEST OF MEXICO

1

The Approach to Montezuma

First we shall go
by helicopter,

then by midget submarine,
then by bubble car,
and finally by

Shanks's pony.

Orlando folds
his wings,
and salutes the rising sun.

2

EXCUSE ME

Is that the Estuary of the Plate?

Sorry, I don't speak
Nahuatl either.

Orlando is stumped.

3

The Monroe Doctrine

Mounting an armadillo
Orlando rides in triumph
into Tenochtitlan.

D

Feathers, gold
ornaments, and
excellent washing facilities

are laid on by the local
Orlando Tourist Board.

4

A Speech by Orlando

If Montezuma
wants it that way,
OK he can have it

BOY, O BOY

will we smack
that little Indian
piss-willy !

5

Orlando incarcerates
Montezuma
in a golden phial.

He then floats it
down the Amazon.

The Amazon bares her breast to receive it.

THOUGHTS OF CHAIRMAN ORLANDO

1

> Never trust a daffodil.

Enjoy bittermints
> only on Sundays.

2

Have a break, have an ORLANDO
You can take an ORLANDO anywhere
ORLANDO is more than a bedtime drink

3

> ORLANDO Swimwear
The new ORLANDO GTE
> Mackintosh's ORLANDO

4

> Be prepared.
Thou shalt not covet.

> HEIL ORLANDO

5

> Power comes
from the mouth of an ORLANDO.
> Treat your ORLANDO
like your sweetheart.
> ORLANDO first
and ask questions afterwards.

6

Thoughts of Chairman Goering

When I hear the word ORLANDO
I reach for my ORLANDO.

AN ORLANDO SOS

1

CALLING ALL ORLANDOS
CALLING ALL ORLANDOS

Do you read me ?

Please proceed at once
       to your nearest
Orlando Recruiting Station.

     The Orlando Society
is being threatened
     by its enemies.

2

     In Studio L1
Sir Karl Orlando
     studies the Swedish glass.

     There is a rustle
in the potted palms.

     OF THAT HOWEVER MORE LATER

All we can say now
     is that it is definitely not
a *Bertrand* Russell.

3

I HAVE NO STATEMENT TO MAKE AS OF THIS TIME
     Orlando added,

as he became DJ of the year
     in Norway.

45

IV
ORLANDO, TRAVELLER IN TIME

ONE OF ORLANDO'S HISTORICAL MOMENTS

1

It was Vienna.

It was 1910.

Everyone was eating Sachertorte
and doing waltzes.

Then Orlando turned up.

BANG BANG
BANG BANG

The street was cleared in no time.

2

Of course,
Freud was still around
(Hi, Sigmund)
Mahler
(Gustav to you)
Adolf Hitler

SSSSSSSSSSS

(Orlando always hisses
the villain)

Peter Behrens – I guess
I'd better check
my references,
I'm not really sure about Peter Behrens –

And, look !
    Here comes Otto Wagner,
architect *extraordinaire*.
    He is helping them re-build
the whole of the Ring
    in red putty.

3

STOP PRESS

The Emperor Franz Josef
has just eaten an egg.

Orlando has become Count Orlando.

And now back to our sponsors.

BUT FIRST ORLANDO IN VIENNA

1

NEWS FLASH

The Vienna Philharmonic
have all resigned in protest.

Orlando has been caught
impersonating
                    the first violin.

2

Meanwhile, sixty years on,
          Orlando sits
in front of the fire

re-living the Battle of Tancredi and Clorinda
          in Mr Monteverdi'a version
on hi-fi.

3

And *now*
back to our sponsors.

THE JULES VERNE ORLANDO

1

Orlando is thinking :

I shall go a journey
          to the centre of Orlando,
and see what's going on there.

2
Pretty dark in here.

          Strike a light, someone.

SHIVERING STILTS !

What a lot of nasty creepy-crawlies.

3
          You are now entering
the famous ORANGE room.

          Here, the ORANGE poet
wrote the original
          perfect
          (and now famous)

          ORANGE POEM.

Orlando gazes in awe.

GOSH, IT'S FUN

          Later,
he meets the giant lizards.

THE CHRISTIAN ORLANDO

1

NEWS FLASH

     Orlando has just been crowned
Orlando the 13th.

2

Considering the importance
     of being the 13th Orlando
it's surprising
there weren't more candidates.

     Orlando himself
was puzzled.

3

Still, when he'd had a walk
     by the Galilee
     and a few loaves and fishes
he got the message.

ISCARIOT SANDWICHES ARE GUARANTEED
  ICEBERG-FRESH

ORLANDO IN THE STONE AGE

1

Look out, here comes a Brontosaurus !

Orlando gets it
with his ray-gun.

KERFLUMP

All that sponge-rubber
and nothing to show for it
except a few punctures.

Orlando was disgusted.

2

The Invention of Fire

Beside his cave
a small furry man
rubs two twigs together.

A spark emerges
from twig 1
and travels fairly rapidly
towards twig 2.

To repeat experiment :
rub two sticks together.

If no fire is produced
rub two more sticks together.

Orlando
throws up his hands
in irritation.

Catching Orlando's hands
the small furry man
rubs them together.

Orange fur is produced.

3
Me OG, you
NIG.

Make hairy together.

OG say yes.

(Clubbing. Yells.)

Make hairy together now?

4
All the Stone Age
I want
is a few peaches
with a bit of guts to them.

Fingering his member
Orlando agreed
with OG.

ORLANDO IN RUSSIA

Now see here, Napoleon,
I mean, Adolf,

the men don't really want to take Moscow

All they need is a good meal
                              a good fuck
and a night in bed with
    Orlando and the Floppsy Bunnies.

ORLANDO SINKS THE ARK ROYAL

1

In the Studio

NERVOUS !
he certainly doesn't look it,

Orlando reflected,
as he watched the giant
sinking the Ark Royal.

2

Meanwhile, the giant
was drawing Orlando
inside his head.

3

TORPEDO LOS !

Carefully drawn dots
compose a peaked cap, the
dungarees of the ratings, and

the rather uneven balloon
issuing from Orlando's mouth.

4

You're right.

THIS IS THE ROY LICHTENSTEIN VERSION

Fourteen times life-size.

E

V
AN ORLANDO WORKSHOP

ORLANDO RECONSTRUCTED

1

What about some more construction
    in the Orlando poems
a critic wrote.

    Well, why not,
(Orlando thought)
    it's a free world,
some say.

2

    Later,
large building blocks
were brought :
       metal rods
rose in dug supports :
       concrete
was poured :
       curtain windows
(best Munich glass)
       hung themselves in frames
just as if Mies
          van der Rohe
was still around.

    HOW ABOUT THAT, THEN
Orlando called
    from the cabin of the big crane.

The critic looked up.
    Not many critics
look up, but
    this one did.

WELL DONE, THOU GOOD AND FAITHFUL SERVANT
    EXCELLENT WORK, LAD
SOCK IT TO THEM, ORLANDO BABY
    he called back.

Orlando, naturally,
was very proud of himself.

AN ORLANDO FRAGMENT

One night, when Orlando was
walking home
                    he thought,

I know, I'll become a werewolf.

AN ORLANDO JOKE

Orlando is always licking himself.

I think he must be made
of ice-cream.

He is a very cool cat.

I SCREAM

This is my Stevie Smith poem
where you can't tell the poem from the patter.

THE ORLANDO COMMERCIAL

1

EEK !

Her legs are caught in something.

          What appalling catastrophe
has trapped and is so
     atrociously torturing
this beautiful naked girl's
legs ?

Why, ORLANDO, of course.

Elusive, exclusive Orlando
          the new seamless nylon
has stolen up in secret
          and caught her in his lure.

2

Orlando yawns.

He is tired of being a fabric.

     He wants out.

Heh, you can't do that
          you'll tear the screen !

The screen tears.

Just shows.

It can't have been made
          of elusive, exclusive ORLANDO
the new seamless nylon.

AN ORLANDO QUESTION

1

HANDS UP ALL THOSE
    WHO'RE HEARTILY SICK
OF THE ORLANDO POEMS

One : a forest of hands

Two : no hands at all

Three : a medium number of hands

2

A Forest of Hands

Orlando closes his book
and curls up in a corner,
    weeping.

3

No Hands at All

Orlando caprioles
round the stage,
    lifting his hat
and hallooing.

4

A Medium Number of Hands

Orlando harangues
the audience, singling out
    individuals

either with hands up or hands down

and generally exhibiting
symptoms of acute displeasure.

5

HANDS UP ALL THOSE
     WHO'RE HEARTILY SICK
OF *THIS* POEM

THE ORLANDO TOP TWENTY

A COMPLETE ORLANDO TECHNIQUE FOR ADULTS
HOW TO SEE ORLANDO ON FIVE DOLLARS A DAY
WHITHER ORLANDO
HOW TO IMPROVE YOUR ORLANDO IN FOUR EASY
LESSONS
AN ORLANDO PRIMER
THE CHARLES ATLAS ORLANDO
SIXTEEN THINGS YOU OUGHT TO KNOW ABOUT
ORLANDO
ORLANDO IN AFRICA
ORLANDO GOES TO THE LOO
MISS ORLANDO, 1970
THE LIFE AND TIMES OF FIELD MARSHAL
VISCOUNT ORLANDO OF ALAMEIN
AN ORLANDO CHAPBOOK
NEWS FROM THE BIGHT OF ORLANDO
OUT AND ABOUT IN ORLANDO
ORLANDO BESIEGES JERSEY CITY
THE HAND-REARED ORLANDO
THE ORLANDO OWNER'S HAND-BOOK
THREE WAYS OF PREPARING ORLANDO
THE SMOKING-ROOM ORLANDO
A GUIDE TO THE AYLESBURY MUSEUM OF ORLANDO
BYGONES

ORLANDO TRIES TO BE DIFFICULT

1

OBJECTION

The Orlando poems are too easy
　　　they just go straight
in one ear and out the other.

　　　Orlando listens
attentively.

　　　Wetting his copying-pencil,
he begins to write :

2

A Geoffrey Hill Poem

　　　Loyola deciduous,
magnificence incarcerate :
　　　winged ignition
gripped through tense rings : Benin

　　　ivories : clothed juice
of white samphire, still remembered

　　　image of decision,

O MY BOY, MY OWN BOY

3

　　　To be distinguished from a fake,
a manufactured Orlando,
　　　Orlando reflected,

　　　has to be computerised.

THE MULTIPLE ORLANDO

ORLANDO
ORLANDO
ORLANDO
ORLANDO
ORLANDO
ORLANDO
ORLANDO
ORLANDO
ORLANDO
ORLANDO

TO BE CONTINUED

THE MUSICAL ORLANDO

1

MIAOW MIAOW

Ten fibreglass werewolves
advance purposefully
on Orlando.

Clustering decoratively
together,
they begin to sing

the National Anthem.

2

Orlando pays
no attention.

He is too busy
with his catalogues
for the

JOHN CAGE RETROSPECTIVE

3

Elsewhere,
the fiendish Japanese
are developing

their eye-openers.

CATARACTS, O CATARACTS

What horny-handed sons of toil we all are !
Orlando carolled,
as he worked the treadle of his sewing-machine.

THE VIRGINIA WOOLF ORLANDO

1

Orlando
unhooks her bra
and gently strokes her nipples.

HMM

'Tisn't a bit exciting
when you *are* one.

2

I was wrong
(Lady Orlando writes)
in my earlier feeling,

if I may use the expression,

about the erogenous zones.

All are available,
responsive ,and may be washed
in fresh soap
and water.

3

SPLASH SPLASH
SPLASH SPLASH

Orlando adjusts
the nozzle of the bidet.

Pushing his pants down
he steps into hot
        erogenous water,

        the first man ever
        to become a female ant-eater.

F

THE FIVE-MINUTE ORLANDO MACBETH

1

ACT 1

    Orlando hails
the wierd sisters
    and rides homes like a maniac.

    Eschewing the
rooky wood, he
    gallops across four blasted heaths
    towards his castle.

    There, washing her hands

    HERE'S YOUR TRAILER

    Lady Orlando
    stands
with harness on her back.

    DUNC'S HERE
    she says

    HI, DUNC
    he calls

2

    Meanwhile, Lady O
screws his courage to the sticking-point
    and they have a stiff night together.

    Pretty probably.

Next, Orlando dips
the bloody dagger
          in his wife's history book

and sets about gilding the faces of the grooms withal.

          UNFORTUNATELY

          it keeps cropping up
          at awkward times
                              like
in his dreams, during banquets, etc.

3

          MOREOVER

          Hired lads
got in to put the
          Macduff fry

out of their misery
          don't help much,

though admittedly going in the catalogue for men.

4

          Finally, it's

          WITCH TIME AGAIN

          and Thane Orlando
runs his eye along the cauldrons

          BAD NEWS THERE, BUD
but
          he takes it like a man

being, as he says,
so far advanced in gore
to return were as tedious as go o'er.

SO

5

ACT V

Drums. Trumpets. Marching trees

and the old woman with her bad scene
about all the perfumes of Arabia
not being a spot-lifter

RIGHT

not of woman born
untimely ripp'd

a hard choice, but
we all know it has to go at last to the goodies

THANK YOU, MAC ORLANDO

and stick his bloody head on the battlements
on your way out, please.

VI
ORLANDO'S SECRET LIFE

ORLANDO AT HOME

1

Today the giants
are in their cautious mood.

They move apart and apart.

Orlando watches.

2

The giants have been
raving
in their time.

One took the other
once, and bounced her,
back and forth

over Orlando's
queasy fur.

ACRIMONY ACRIMONY

The air crackled with it.

3

BUT WAIT

One of the giants
shall have a baby
the size of a tam-tam.

All flat,
and in the mind.

Orlando promises.

ORLANDO'S LOVE LIFE

1

The scene
is a bent attic bedroom
somewhere in Hampstead.

Overhead
the German bombers
drone home,

I LOVE YOU, I LOVE YOU
screams Orlando.

Well, wouldn't you,
with a 27-year-old
undischarged schizophrenic
holding a bread knife
over your balls ?

2

KNOCK KNOCK
KNOCK KNOCK

Who's there ?

Colonel Orlando
has come, Madam.

Well, I haven't,
so tell him to keep on knocking.

(aside) The insolence
of these military people !

3

Orlando, though,
had a high opinion
of the love-relationship.

He knew quite a few
of the best people in the business
for fornicating.

O yes,
Orlando loves them all,
the red, the white and the khaki.

Only one little lady
with a mouth the size of *The Aspern Papers*
has his heart in her honeysuckle, though.

ORLANDO'S LOVE LIFE, PART TWO

(from the Orlando Apocrypha)

1

Anyway,
that was Mini's view.

Spinning Mini
spends a penny
buying contraceptives for Orlando
whenever she gets the chance.

Orlando kills so many babies
every Sunday
there isn't room to put the carcases
in a concentration camp.

According to Mini.

2

Never be a Mini.
It lives in a hot-house
and eats rhododendrons
according to Orlando.

When you pick it up
by the ears
it nips your finger
with its bad temper.

It has a very dry
bad temper.

Orlando once spent
a whole winter
sprinkling weed-killer on it.

83

3

    Proper names
make improper poems.

    This had better be
the first
       UNDERGROUND
Orlando poem.

ORLANDO AND THE DARK LADY

1

Orlando is very sad.

He sits weeping
into his beef tea.

AH ME, THE YEARS, THE YEARS

Down his cold cheek
the rain-drop ploughs.

2

How shall we treat
with the dark lady of these sonnets,
given that she is wall-eyed,

eats beans, and lives in a hovel ?

Orlando has no idea.

Here it is very dark
and the dark lady
is going away into the dark.

Outside it snows with children
neither of them can catch
without one melting.

ORLANDO VISITS THE UNDERWORLD

1

Every day
Orlando's father is in the garden
recognisable by his black tail.

Orlando sleeps
in the airing-cupboard.

It may be as hot
as hell in there, but
Orlando loves it.

2

When Orlando poured
a libation of orange juice
the dead

all came out of their daffodils
and groaned in unison :

I AM THY FATHER'S GHOST, ORLANDO

Only none of them was,
not one.

BLOODY LIARS

The whole thing was done with mirrors.

3

It would take more
than a bit of liver
to get Orlando eating
his mother's death.

The dead enjoy liver
about as much as the living
        like chalk.

        Orlando's mother
was no exception, she was just
        Orlando's mother.

        For her he cries
not often, but sometimes.

        Her he remembers
when she comes and growls at him
        from the architect's table.

4

        Orlando's mother
and father,
        they make a fine pair

in the photograph of their honeymoon
for 1926.

ORLANDO AT THERMOPYLAE

1

Aeroplanes are making
their usual noise
on the way to Runway Number 4

ONLY

There is no way in,
or out either,
for poor Orlando.

The Persians are all around him.

2

A Persian Song

Sing a song of six poets
porraged in a pie.

One laughed, one died,
One rhymed, and one cried :

Sing a song of two poets
flying in the sky
                    HOOP

LA !

3

Everybody is laughing
except Orlando.

Orlando is crying
up someone else's sleeve.

And the Spartans
are still holding the pass,

where Orlando is dying.

ORLANDO ON A WET SUNDAY

1

Somewhere Orlando
has missed his connection.

He has grown
small enough
to drown in a teardrop.

2

Last Train to Roncesvalles

Swords and fishes
compete
for a place in the window.

Orlando sits
on a knife-edge,
tipping the scales.

3

Could do with a pint, sir

Dip-stick shows
you're a bit short
on spermatozoa

ZUM ZUM
ZUM ZUM

The scimitar goes into the sunset.

VII
ORLANDO SAYS GOODBYE

THE LAST DAYS OF ORLANDO

1

A whispering campaign has started
against Orlando.

By the middle of June
he may have to go
into exile.

I DON'T WANT TO GO INTO EXILE

(Shut up, Orlando,
who's writing this poem,
you or me)

In July
there will be a march.

Banners. Demonstrations.

On August the 13th
a question will be asked
in the House of Representatives.

Leaflets advocating
the forcible withdrawal
of all our Orlandos

East of Suez
will be hurled
from the Public Galleries.

2

Now it is September.

A small force
of dedicated men

creeps through a jungle
somewhere in Malaya

STEADY ON, LADS

A rustle in the undergrowth.

LOOK OUT. HERE HE COMES.

and the last living Orlando
crashes through the bush
with a British bullet in his brain.

I'D RATHER KILL A CHINESE
THAN AN ORLANDO, ANY DAY

SON OF ORLANDO

1

The title
is a misnomer.

Far better would be
It Always Rains in Orlando.

Particularly on Sundays.

2

Dear Father :

I am alive and well and shining
in South Molesden.

Most of our friends
keep their blinds down.

Still, I shall rise again.

Signed : Orlando

3

Very treacherous brute
your Orlando.

Never tell when
you've got him.

YES, I'LL HAVE A SUNDOWNER

ORLANDO RIDES AGAIN

1

       This is the BIG picture.

       In it, Orlando
confronts his arch-enemy
       the notorious Luigi Pulci.

       Luigi is big meat
in the mafia – don't mess
       with *him* is right.

       Anyway, Orlando
has the better of it
       in cantos one, three and seven.

       Two, six and eight
are drawn :
       heavy breathing,
both men stretch on the canvas,
       this is a GAY picture

       That leaves rounds four, five
and nine.

       These were Luigi's.

       NOW READ ON

2

Round Ten

       Very light
on his pins, this little medieval fighter

nippy as a night-jar
mean as a weasel

MANALIVE

Ain't a gonna be
a mafia champ no more if

he
has his way.

3
SLUG SLUG
SLUG SLUG

Still round ten.

Luigi has just
tried a new trick,
trapped Orlando
in a really dirty series of *ottava rima*

WOW

He never saw that one coming

(Orlando tucks
his inter-exponential callisthenic super-Missal missile
back in his pocket.)

It helps to know the Pope.

Luigi is out cold.

4

Dirge

     According to his lights,
he was a good man,
       invented the giants,

       opened the first soup-kitchens,
attended the funeral
       of Al Capone.

SING ALONG
SING ALONG

This is the Luigi
Pulci song.

Orlando sheds his tear in the appropriate receptacle.

ORLANDO'S LAST BATTLE

1

Propped up
on a Victorian chaise-longue
with a glass of hot toddy in his paw

Orlando dictates
his Last Will and Testament.

To my fellow-sufferers I bequeath :

piles, ear-ache, nostalgia,
gripe, and Egyptian tummy

To all who were with me
in the ships at Mylae

my signed copy
of *The Waste Land*

(Ezra's fingerprints in the left hand margin)

To Peter Behrens

my apologies –

it wasn't 1910
it wasn't Vienna

2

Well, so much for that,
Orlando thought,

dusting off the Felix grains
from the bedspread.

Now we can get down
to the real meat.

WHO'S NEXT FOR THE KNACKER'S YARD

3

Envoi

The light failing,
or seeming to,
Orlando took his olifant and sword again,

DURENDAL, of which he was proud,

and fed it through
the mincing-machine.

This they would never get, at any rate.

AN ORLANDO RETROSPECTIVE

1

OCHRE-BALLED ORLANDO

Proper little Casanova,
he was.

He'd be about
327 years old
if he were alive today.

Just think of that now.

2

A plate smashes
in smithereens
against the door of the ORANGE room.

They still call it
the Orlando syndrome.

3

A Note from the Yellow Press

The Orlando syndicate
has tested all the available data
without success.

None of the synthetic Orlandos
can even speak Italian.

THE CHE GUEVARA ORLANDO

1

Orlando dreams
of Orlando.

In his dream
he swings in the trees again,

free of disease,

eats bananas,
beats his chest,

itches his bottom, examines his finger nails,

wrestles with his keeper

according to Julian Huxley
is the most magnificent animal
that ever was

and guys no one

So three cheers (they say
in the dream)
for

ORLANDO ORLANDO ORLANDO

whose brain is as big as a man's.

2

And three more (they say
in the woods)
for

CHE CHE CHE

whose balls are as big as an ape's.